DUNE BUGGIES

Sarah Tieck

Amazing Vehicles

ABDO
Publishing Company

VISIT US AT
www.abdopublishing.com

Published by ABDO Publishing Company, 8000 West 78th Street, Edina, Minnesota 55439.

Printed in the United States.

Coordinating Series Editor: Rochelle Baltzer
Contributing Editors: Heidi M.D. Elston, Megan M. Gunderson, BreAnn Rumsch, Marcia Zappa
Graphic Design: Deb Coldiron, Marcia Zappa
Cover Photograph: Justin Anderson
Interior Photographs/Illustrations: Justin Anderson (pp. 5, 12, 14, 16, 22); Melissa Anderson (p. 17); *AP Photo*: Jacques Brinon (p. 23), Pablo Martinez Monivais (p. 27), Chris Pondy/Yuma Daily Sun (p. 5), Tim Tadder (p.13); *Fotosearch*: Corbis (p. 15), Value Stock Images (p. 29); *Getty Images*: Alan Band/Fox Photos (p. 29), TORSTEN BLACKWOOD/AFP (p. 30), Gareth Cattermole (p. 21), Kevin Winter (p. 21); Brian Glass (p. 9); *iStockphoto*: ©iStockphoto/DIGIcal (p. 7), ©iStockphoto/MAYBAYBUTTER (p. 9), ©iStockphoto/nickfree (p. 19), ©iStockphoto/urosr (p. 7); *Shutterstock*: risteski goce (p. 11), Len Green (p. 10), urosr (p. 7); *U.S. Navy*: Photographers Mate 1st Class Arlo Abrahamson (p. 25); *Wikipedia.org* (p. 19).

Library of Congress Cataloging-in-Publication Data

Tieck, Sarah, 1976-
  Dune buggies / Sarah Tieck.
    p. cm. -- (Amazing vehicles)
  ISBN 978-1-60453-541-9
  1. Dune buggies--Juvenile literature. I. Title.

TL236.7.T54 2009
629.222--dc22

                        2009001756

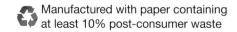
Manufactured with paper containing
at least 10% post-consumer waste

CONTENTS

Dune buggies are commonly used in sand dunes, or hills. That's how they got their name. They are also called beach buggies and sand rails.

GET MOVING

Imagine riding in a dune buggy. Warm air blows past as you bounce over sand hills. It is easy to cover a lot of ground in a short time!

Have you ever looked closely at a dune buggy? Many parts work together to make it move. A dune buggy is an amazing vehicle!

Some dune buggy drivers do tricks, such as wheelies. A wheelie is when the driver pops the front tires off the ground.

WHAT IS A DUNE BUGGY?

Dune buggies are **recreational** vehicles. They are used on and off roads.

Dune buggies have large tires. This helps them move easily over unsteady surfaces. So, people often drive dune buggies on beaches and in deserts.

Dune buggies are often very different from each other. Most are specially built using a range of parts.

Many people build their own dune buggies. They use old car parts or building kits. Some dune buggies are made at factories and then sold. Popular dune buggy models are the Meyers Manx, the Burro, and the EMPI Sportster.

Many people use old Volkswagen Beetles (*left*) as the basis for dune buggies.

Dune buggies (*right*) can be made up of frames and parts from most types of cars. People choose parts based on how the dune buggy will be used.

A CLOSER LOOK

A dune buggy can have an open frame or a **fiberglass** body. It is easy to see the chassis on an open-frame dune buggy. The chassis is the buggy's frame and working parts.

Since the 1960s, many dune buggies have been built with fiberglass bodies. On this type of dune buggy, fiberglass covers most of the chassis.

DUNE BUGGIES

 Roll bars help protect riders in open-frame dune buggies.

 A **steering wheel** allows the driver to guide the direction of the dune buggy.

 The seats have strong **seat belts** to help protect riders.

 Fiberglass bodies give dune buggies a sporty look. They also help protect the riders.

 Dune buggies have wide **tires**. A tire's outer layer is called tread. The pattern in the tread helps the tire move over uneven surfaces.

HOW DOES IT MOVE?

A dune buggy's parts work together to make it move. First, its engine supplies the force to turn its **axles**. The axles connect to the dune buggy's wheels. The spinning axles turn the wheels. This makes the dune buggy move!

A dune buggy can move in different directions. To control its direction, the driver turns a **steering** wheel.

A dune buggy's wide tires help it move easily over sand. But, some dune buggies can also drive on city streets!

POWERFUL ENGINES

Many dune buggies have powerful engines, like those in large cars. A powerful engine can move a dune buggy really fast!

Most dune buggy engines run on a **fuel** called gasoline. The fuel burns inside the engine. This makes the power that moves the dune buggy.

A dune buggy's engine is often located at the back of the vehicle.

Seat belts and helmets help protect drivers. But, drivers must also travel at safe speeds.

DRIVER'S SEAT

Driving a dune buggy uses many of the same skills as driving a car. So, in some cases a **license** is required.

It is important that drivers use their dune buggies safely. Certain dune buggies are made for kids. They can ride more safely in these than in adult dune buggies. Riders of all ages should wear seat belts and helmets.

BUGGY MADNESS

Dune buggies first became popular in the 1960s. Around this time, Bruce Meyers created the Meyers Manx. This was the first vehicle to be widely known as a dune buggy.

Soon, people worldwide owned these sporty vehicles. They came in colorful, fun models. People drove them off road on sunny beaches. Some drove them on streets, too!

People still drive dune buggies with the original Meyers Manx style. And, there is a modern version called the Manxter 2+2.

ON THE SCREEN

In the late 1960s, dune buggies began appearing in movies and television. They were in the 1968 film *The Thomas Crown Affair*. The actors rode in a Meyers Manx.

In the 1970s, a dune buggy was in the Spider-Man comic book. And in 1973, the cartoon *Speed Buggy* featured a talking dune buggy.

Dune buggies continue to appear in movies and television shows. They also appear in music videos and video games.

The dune buggy in the Spider-Man comic book was called the Spider-Mobile. Spider-Man and a friend built it. It looked like a Meyers Manx.

Famous rapper Nelly rode in a dune buggy during an MTV special.

SPEED RACER

Dune buggies are used in many races. Championship Off Road Racing (CORR) is one racing league with several events. Drivers **compete** in off-road races. They speed around racetracks and jump over hills!

Dune buggy races are popular around the world. The Race of Champions is a yearly event. It features Indy car, NASCAR, and Formula One drivers racing dune buggies.

ON THE JOB

Dune buggies can even help people with work. The military uses dune buggies. They help soldiers move quickly. And, they turn easily on off-road surfaces.

The U.S. Navy SEALs is one military group that uses dune buggies. Their buggies are called Desert Patrol Vehicles (DPVs).

DPVs are stocked with the latest military weapons and technology.

25

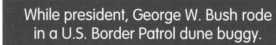
While president, George W. Bush rode in a U.S. Border Patrol dune buggy.

The U.S. Border Patrol also uses dune buggies. Patrollers drive them near the country's borders. They make sure no one enters illegally.

In the 1970s, lifeguards used dune buggies. They drove them while on patrol. These vehicles could quickly carry lifeguards and supplies to help swimmers.

UNITED STATES
BORDER PATROL

Z3517

27

PAST TO PRESENT

In the 1920s, buggies were simple and lightweight. They were made for off-road driving. New models called dune buggies appeared in the 1960s. These popular, colorful vehicles were spotted on beaches and roads everywhere.

Today, dune buggies are still driven throughout the world. Some cruise on streets and beaches. Others race or help with important work. Dune buggies are amazing vehicles!

Some modern dune buggies look very much like older models. But, the engines and parts are always being improved.

BLAST FROM THE PAST

Many dune buggies are made for tough, off-road travel. In 1972, brothers Ed and Bob Turnham set out to show this. They drove Meyers Manx dune buggies across Australia's Simpson Desert.

This was a daring trip. It covered more than 800 miles (1,300 km). There were no **paved** roads. Plus, the desert gets very hot. Still, the brothers made it across. They proved that dune buggies can handle tough conditions.

IMPORTANT WORDS

axle (AK-suhl) a bar on which a wheel or a pair of wheels turns.

compete to take part in a contest between two or more persons or groups.

fiberglass a material made of plastic and very fine fibers of glass.

fuel (FYOOL) something burned to give heat or power.

license (LEYE-suhnts) a paper or a card showing that someone is allowed to do something by law.

paved covered with a material, such as tar, to make a level surface for travel.

recreational (reh-kree-AY-shuh-nuhl) of or relating to an activity done in free time for fun or enjoyment.

steering relating to guiding or controlling a moving vehicle.

WEB SITES

To learn more about dune buggies, visit ABDO Publishing Company online. Web sites about dune buggies are featured on our Book Links page. These links are routinely monitored and updated to provide the most current information available.

www.abdopublishing.com

INDEX